Think and Grow Forward

10 Strategies for Personal Empowerment

Michele Sfakianos, RN, BSN

Open Pages Publishing, LLC

http://www.openpagespublishing.com

Copyright © 2019 by Michele Sfakianos, RN, BSN

ISBN 978-1-7322722-4-8

Printed in the United States of America

Photo credit: ID 114956835 © Khwanchai Phanthong | Dreamstime.com

Disclaimer

The information in this book is:

- of a general nature and not intended to address the specific circumstances of any particular individual or entity;
- written as a guide and is not intended to be a comprehensive tool, but is complete, accurate, or up to date at the time of writing;
- an information tool only and not intended to be used in place of a visit, consultation, or advice of a medical professional;

This book is not intended to serve as professional or legal advice (if you need specific advice, you should always consult a suitably qualified professional).

This book is dedicated to those who are willing to put in the hard work to "grow-forward" in their purpose to create an empowered life.
I believe in you. You can do this!

Foreword

Highly successful entrepreneur, business and personal coach, and international speaker, Michele Sfakianos is honored to bring you her strategies on how to enhance your life. Michele teaches individuals, organizations and companies how to achieve their desired results by recognizing and applying their own unique learning model for achievement. Michele is a master at helping people uncover their true potential and define their purpose, mentoring them in the direction of their dreams. Think and Grow Forward is the culmination of Michele's study and work in the field of personal development. In these 10 chapters, Michele will help you to create your own learning model for achievement. She explores basic virtues of honesty and courage, and strategies such as focus and leadership to help you "grow forward" towards your life's vision and purpose.

Table of Contents

Understanding

Before I jump into the introduction and the first strategy of Understanding, I want to tell you something. I talk pretty openly about my faith in this book and will quote scripture from time to time. I do that because it has been an important part of my personal journey. It may also be a part of yours. But I also know that it may not be. Rest assured I will not try to force my faith on you. I sincerely believe you'll benefit from hearing this information.

So, let's jump into it. Some of you may know a little bit about my background, and some of you may not. So, let me give you the "readers digest version". I was born in Homestead, Florida in a traditional American family. I was raised in a middle-class family by both parents until they divorced when I was fifteen. I lived with my mom after the divorce and continued to receive support from both parents in everything I did.

I married at age 19, while in college. Graduated college and was six weeks pregnant, so I never was able to get a job in my field. Within 27 months of marriage, I had two children. I got a divorce by age 26 and it was at that time I found myself in a difficult situation. I was recently divorced, had two small children ages 3 and 5, and wasn't sure how I was going to make ends meet without the security of another paycheck. I knew needed to find a job that paid well, even though I was getting child support, but had a hard time finding work. I had a college degree, but hadn't really worked in that field, so no one would hire me because I didn't have any experience. So, I picked up the newspaper and all of the jobs that paid well seemed to be in Nursing. After thinking about it for several weeks, I called the local college to see how many of my credits would transfer from one degree to another. I also talked to my mom about moving back home so she could help me with the kids while I went back to school.

I ended up working three part-time jobs and going to school full-time to become a Registered Nurse. It took me about two and half years, but I did it. It took me a little longer because I had to relocate my home and school due to Hurricane Andrew (but that's another story!). The bottom line is I set my sight on something that would take care of me and children and I did it. There were many nights I wanted to give up, but I knew I would be a better person, role model and mother if I could just complete this degree.

So, I worked as a Registered Nurse for three years and felt that there had to be more to life – more that I could do for a larger amount of people. I went into Nurse Recruitment and then Nursing Informatics, where I spent the next 18 years programming clinical software used in hospitals. That certainly helped thousands of staff and patients, but there was still something missing.

I remarried eight years later. Raising two children on my own wasn't easy, but with this new person in my life, he was definitely a wonderful addition. My focus was always my children and how to make their life better. However, along the way, I realized that instead of teaching my children how to live on their own, I was doing everything for them. I was what they call an "enabler". It was at that time I knew I needed to make changes. My son had already moved out, but my daughter was still at home and now a single mother. She wanted to move out on her own, which terrified me because I wasn't sure I had taught her everything she needed to know to not only take care of herself, but to take care of my grandson as well. So, I started making notes for her. It was at that time I realized I had a passion for writing and wrote my first book entitled

"Useful Information for Everyday Living" – which is now "The 4-1-1 on Life Skills" and "Ace Your Life – Life Management Skills Made Easy."

After writing eight books, I realized I had a knack for helping others. I then started to gravitate to more self-help and motivational books and thought it would be great to be a motivational speaker or a life coach. So, I found myself becoming a really avid student and reader in the field of human potential. I've read a lot of books. But, see, in all of that reading, I just couldn't get any information to really stick to help me make a change. Now some of it stuck, don't get me wrong. I would find myself getting motivated, but no permanent change. Once I completed reading the book or listening to the program the motivation stopped after a few weeks and sometimes even just after days. Have you experienced that? You go to a seminar, get really motivated, and then go home and days later you are back in the same rut and the motivation is gone.

It was at that point I knew I needed a completely new direction. I did not need motivation; I needed some understanding – a better under-standing of how to achieve. And part of the understanding that I received I'm going to share with you in this book. And without a doubt in my mind, the understanding I received from the strategies in this book literally changed me and every area of my life.

You know, we can hear somebody say that something changed their life, and almost, as a passive listener, it becomes hard to believe unless you've experienced it. I always knew I had the potential to build a busi-ness; I just lacked the awareness and belief and these strategies that I'm going to share.

You see, I lacked the awareness of my potential. I always felt that I was put here on this earth to do great things, but didn't know how to accomplish them. I lacked a certain belief in myself that I could actually do it. I saw potential in other people and other things, not so much in myself. My goal here for you is to understand these strategies or big ideas in a really meaningful way, in an authentic way.

I'm not necessarily worried if I communicate perfectly. What I mean by this is I get so excited sharing this information with you that from time to time it may seem as if I "speak" too fast! Just hang in there with me! What I want to do is - I want to connect with you. And I've purposely kept each chapter short. I want you to be able to read them and get some real understanding. There are lots of books on the market today that have a lot of fluff. I've intentionally made this short and given as much true content as I possibly can.

This book of key strategies will not only transform your method of achieving your goals, and dreams, but will also shift your old traditional beliefs and judgments. I know all of the strategies will shape your learning model process of achieving the life you desire, the life you deserve, the life that is rightfully yours to claim, a fully rewarding and successful life.

Each concept will open the door to a new awareness and guide you with daily practices that tear down the walls of limiting ideas that prevented you from your full achievement and a beautiful, successful life. The strategies will change your decision-making ability, which will change your life as you see it and how you live it today. These ideas will wash away your fears that you don't deserve, or that you can't achieve your true desires, and will enhance your visions beyond your wildest dreams. Success can and will be yours.

So, why do I call these strategies? Well, I've learned and tested each of these strategies through experience, and I personally formed a successful, rewarding life using them. And for me, that's powerful. And let me help you understand the idea of the strategies. I've learned the way we do everything in our life is really based on a learning model that is created by our awareness, belief, and understanding that we have of these strategies. These learning models are ultimately maintained or supported by our conditioning and our habits.

The way we get dressed in the morning, the way you tie your shoes, the way you put your pants on, the way you drive your car, the way you make decisions, the way we interact with our loved ones and our coworkers, the way we make decisions about maintaining our body temple, our eating habits, our physical activity – all of this operates through learning models.

As I became aware of the understanding of why we do what we do and why we don't do some of the things that we really want to do, I realized that these learning models are based on three things.

First, it is based on our level of awareness of our potential, the awareness of the opportunities right in front of us, and the awareness of maybe future pitfalls, obstacles, or challenges that we may face in our lives.

For most of our lifetimes, we were programmed to believe that we had to be in the right place at the right time if we were going to succeed. I found that to be a lie, because I know in my life – and perhaps you've experienced this too – that in my life, there have been times when I was smack dab in the middle of exactly the right place, at exactly the right time, and while everybody around me was winning and I was losing.

See, it's not just about being in the right place at the right time. We are always in the right place at the right time. It's about having the awareness of your potential while you're there. I have found without awareness of our potential; we can absolutely be in the right place at the right time and not see the opportunities right in front of us.

Once you begin to master the strategies within a learning model of achievement, you will find even if you are in the wrong place at the wrong time, you can succeed, because the potential for winning is with you always. Now, you can find people who are saying that currently we are in a down economy or a down market, and this is the wrong time to grow a business or take a risk. And while everyone else is playing it safe, as you expand your awareness of your potential, your self-belief, and you begin to apply these strategies, you're going to find that you can win regardless of the conditions and circumstances.

So, as you will see – it has very little to do with being in the right place at the right time, and it has everything to do with being aware of your potential, believing in your ability to do it, and to master the strategies that I'm going to share with you throughout this entire book.

The second component of the learning model is based on our current level of belief. What do you really believe you are capable of achieving your life? In a phenomenal book by Dr. Maxwell Maltz entitled Psycho-Cybernetics, he clearly states that a person does not get what it is that they want in their life, that what they get in their life is what they think they are capable of achieving, what they believe. He says a person cannot outperform their own self-image.

You see, that's what happened to me. The reason I was stuck wasn't because of the economy; it wasn't because of my customers. It had nothing to do with my employees. What happened was that I had reached the level of my self-belief, and I never believed myself able or capable of outperforming. So, I sabotaged every opportunity to grow and move forward until I learned to change that belief, that self-image. I expanded my awareness of my potential, as I began to apply these strategies.

So, how we do everything is really based on a learning model. And that learning model, again, is based on our awareness and our current beliefs. And within each learning model, there are strategies that we must master in order to call that learning model successful. See, even if we expand our awareness, even if we have belief, if we don't learn to master the strategies within the model that we're developing, we develop a learning model of failure.

Let me give you an example of a learning model that I think we can all relate to. There was probably a time in your life where you had a really strong desire to ride a bicycle, but your personal learning model at that time was probably a learning model of failure. You got on by yourself, but you lacked the awareness and understanding of your potential and all the strategies within the learning model to ride the bicycle.

You lacked the belief in your ability to be able to ride the bike, even though you saw your sister or your brother or a neighbor or friend ride the bike. And in order for that learning model of failure to be transformed to a learning model where you are now successfully riding a bike, several things had to happen. First there was a coach or mentor. That was probably your mom or dad, or an older brother or a sister who stood beside you while you sat on the bike. And they began to expand your awareness of your potential. They began to share with you a new belief that you could actually do it. You, in effect, borrowed their belief.

Then they started to teach you some of the strategies about riding the bike with the next learning model. They probably talked to you about balance and hand/eye coordination and muscle dexterity. And as they stood beside you on the bike and ran beside you as you pedaled and pushed, they let you go. And chances are you fell. But you recognized that you did pedal one or two times. And although you didn't fully believe you could do it, you decided to act on the borrowed belief of your coach or mentor. So, you got back on the bike.

And again, they began to expand your understanding of the strategies, helped you gain an awareness of your potential that you could really do it, and you borrowed their belief. They showed you what you did wrong. They encouraged you to do it better, and they helped you master the strategies. Each time in the process of failing and getting back on the bike, you expanded your awareness of your potential. You gained a better understanding of the strategies, and you changed your limiting belief that said, "You can do this," to, "I can do this."

Now, for most of us, in a very short period of time, we learned how to ride a bike. And that learning model still sticks with us for the rest of our lives. As I've had the privilege and opportunity of working with very successful individuals, from all walks of life and fields of endeavor, I've looked at their lives. I've been very curious about, "What are the strategies within the learning model for their life achievement? What is it that these people had that seemingly others lacked?" Then I came to realize that they were operating with key strategies, and that's why I call these strategies.

Take a look at your life. Look at the areas of your life where you've been really successful. You're going to find these ten strategies were properly applied in your life in that area. I intend to show you how to change your learned behavior and any limiting self-judgments that you may have bought into with counterfeit thoughts. The illustration I give you about riding a bike is a basic understanding. But what about something bigger, something greater than just riding a bike without training wheels? What about creating a learning model of achievement for your entire life? What would it be like to change your entire life so you were living your ultimate dream?

Now, that takes us to a whole new dimension, which is the third process for the learning model. Ask yourself, "Am I really ready for this? Am I really, really ready?" See, once we self-author or create a mental model of perfection that we want for our lives, that becomes the first process for us to reach our goal.

You know, for me and my life, I knew I could change my life, but wasn't aware of how. For years I remained stuck. My learning model and beliefs said that if I was to be successful, that I needed to have more money and a team of people. And my awareness of my potential, based on that belief, produced a result. My learning model, my belief and awareness said that it takes money to make money. Well, I didn't have any money to make any money. My learning model, based on my belief and awareness said that it's better to be safe than sorry. So, I didn't dare bet on myself. *I* was way too much of a risk.

The truth is, in order for any of us to achieve success in life it requires taking a risk. So, my result was I settled for feeling stuck in every area of my life. Part of my learning model said that I had to play the hand I was dealt based on my awareness and belief. Perhaps you've been told that, too. I found out that it's not true. I found out that not only can we throw our hand that we were dealt back to the center for the table, if we choose to; we can gain understanding, expand our awareness of our potential, and move beyond the convictions of our limiting belief. If we begin to study and gain an understanding of the strategies in our life, we can become the dealer of the cards in our own life.

This adventure is not a fishing trip, where you're equipped with all the necessary gear, but you have no guarantee of catching a fish. This is the journey that begins with understanding that you, as an individual, truly are equipped with all the necessary gear, all the resources necessary to co-create a life beyond the condition and circumstances you find yourself in. It has nothing to do with hope and everything to do with belief. This is your chance – for all of us. We get one chance here on Earth. Remember, this is not a dress rehearsal. You have been gifted with all the resources to create the life that you truly want and deserve.

It was my intention in creating this book, and my highest hope for you, to gain a deeper understanding of these truths within each of the strategies and gain fortitude, faith, and belief in your ability to create your authentic, successful, rewarding life. Believe in yourself and believe in your ability to achieve. You have mastered many individual challenges in your lifetime. Now is the time to master your life. This is why I believe the first strategy is Understanding.

In Proverbs 3:13 it says, "Blessed is the man who finds wisdom, the man who gains understanding." See, there's a difference between knowing and wisdom. There are a lot of people in our lives who say they know something, and all of us know how to do better things in our lives, myself included. I love to eat frozen custard. Just because I love doing this doesn't mean it is good for me (or my waist line!).

Most sales people know that if they simply ask for referrals and stay connected with their prospects and customers, they'll increase their sales. But they don't always do what they know. Most people know, in relation-ships with our loved ones, that if we started our day and ended each day looking into the eyes of those people who are most important in our lives and tell them that we love them, that we care about them and how significant they are to us, those relationships would deepen. But we don't always do what we know.

It's been said that the largest gap in our life is the gap between that which we know and that which we do. And I believe the bridge between the gap of knowing and doing is understanding. When we know something, typically that's a process of gathering information, like we were taught to do in school: read, remember, repeat; read, remember, repeat. Then we can say we know because we've answered a certain number of questions on a quiz.

Understanding requires internalizing the knowledge, stepping out and acting on the knowledge, understanding the change and the feedback of our results and the conditions/circumstances in our environment, and then making the necessary adjustments in that process.

All of my study has convinced me that the only way we gain true understanding of anything is through a two-step process of study and application. And that's what you'll be doing in this book. You'll study each of the strategies and become emotionally involved with them. You'll do what Motivational Speaker Zig Ziglar says – you know, a "check up from the neck up" with each of the strategies. You can evaluate each of the strategies in relationship to your own life. And then, with each strategy, I will share some simple things you can do to apply that understanding to your life.

So, you will see what begins to change in your life from that experience. You can ask yourself, "How do I apply this in new strategy to my learning? To what area of my life? How does this change my conditions? How does this change my circumstances? What is the feedback that I've gotten from this?" You know, sometimes we define the feedback as failure.

Sometimes we define the feedback as success. The truth is it's neither success nor failure; it's feedback that allows us to reevaluate and make the necessary adjustments. And then take the next step forward in our life.

If I've learned anything through my understanding of these strategies, it's that the conditions and circumstances of our lives can never, and will never, predict what is possible in our lives. This is why we've been gifted with imagination: our ability to co-create the mental model of perfection beyond the limiting circumstances and conditions we find ourselves in, and into a fuller expansion of our lives.

As far as we know it, in this entire universe, you and I are the only beings, the only creatures that have been gifted with this power of imagination, with this power to create a life beyond our conditions and circumstances. This may sound silly, but it's true. You'll never drive down a road in Georgia and pass a field of cows and see one of the cows jump up on the fence post and say to the other cows, "Hey, listen. You know, we don't have to be cows anymore; we can be giraffes or kangaroos. We can be dogs. We don't have to just be cows." See, they don't have the ability to change their lives.

You and I, every single moment of every single day, have been gifted with the ability to change. You know, for me, for so many years, I didn't believe this. I wasn't aware of my potential, and I didn't understand the strategies of how to do it. See, when we say, "I can no longer accept this for my life," is when we begin to co-create. We begin to work with the power that I define as God – G-O-D – the Grand Overall Designer. Some of you may refer to this power as universal intelligence, or infinite power or energy. But you're going to hear me in this book define this creative source as God.

I've come to know this, that there is a power that we can co-create our lives with. When we expand our awareness of our infinite true potential; when we challenge the convictions of our old limiting beliefs and replace them with new empowering beliefs; when we gain a true understanding of who we are and, more importantly, *whose* we are and apply the Strategies in our lives, we will never again be held in the field of limitation of what we currently have and see for our lives.

Understanding

NOTES

Honesty

From childhood, we've all been in situations where we've had to make choices about whether to behave honestly or to be less than truthful. As kids, these may have ranged from taking change from our mother's purse to lying to spare ourselves punishment. And as adults, we may have fibbed to spare someone's feelings or deducted a little bit more than we were entitled to on our tax returns.

While we tend to give a lot of lip service to honesty, the daily news has shown us, for example, that a growing number of young people think that it's okay to cheat in school, that every day more drivers are regularly exceeding the speed limit by more than ten miles an hour, and hardly any parent would think it wrong to buy an adult movie ticket for their pre-teen. The problem remains that these kinds of minor transgressions are done without any remorse. We tend to justify and rationalize our actions because "everybody's doing it," or, "it's really not hurting anyone."

In fact, this might be the worst type of dishonesty: not to recognize the absolute nature of honesty, operating on the assumption that there are different standards of honesty. We end up cheating our own personal integrity that lies within us. We are draining our personal power and cheating ourselves and others.

The concept of honesty has depth like an ocean, and it must be properly understood and internalized before we can meaningfully move on to the other strategies for success. Although we're often exposed to examples of dishonesty in media, society as a whole has long celebrated honesty's virtues. For instance, who hasn't heard the line that honesty is the best policy, or the folk tale of George Washington cutting down the cherry tree and proclaiming, "I cannot tell a lie"?

Great writers have often written and spoken about the virtue of honesty as well. The 18th century poet Alexander Pope declared that an honest man is the noblest of God's work. And in the depths of the Great Depression, President Roosevelt said, in his first inaugural address, that it was "no wonder that confidence was in such short supply, for there was little honor and honesty to bolster it."

While these more traditional references to honesty are an important part of our history, I want to explore this fundamental virtue a little deeper, not as a behavior, but as a personal attribute. You see, honesty is a lot more than not lying or speaking untruths. These things represent honesty's most conventional and superficial layer. Honesty is far richer than this. It is a way to be with yourself, with your intentions, and with others. Here lies the confidence and the nobility of honesty that we saw in the words of Alexander Pope and President Roosevelt.

This core honesty has deep roots and a direct correlation to the results in your life. Without honesty, nothing can exist properly, and nothing can be sustained. There's no foundation, but when we live according to, or within the concept of honesty, our power multiples.

So, let's look more fully at what honesty means and what it doesn't. We can define honesty as the quality of being truthful and sincere, of being morally correct or virtuous, of being free of deceit, of being genuine. Yet there is also such a thing as being brutally honest in a way that needlessly hurts other people. I think all of us understand this kind of abrasiveness and we do our best not to hurt the feelings of others. We can still seek honesty that is in keeping with our own higher awareness and reality, but is also kind and not unnecessarily harsh. Honesty is not an excuse to say or do things that shouldn't be said or done, and it should never be a justification to be abrasive or tactless.

So, to move forward in our lives, we must have the awareness and be in harmony with honesty within ourselves in our own lives. And you know, unfortunately, dishonesty is everywhere in our society. And one of its most common forms is often found within an individual. You know, an example of this type of dishonesty is addiction. It could be of drugs, alcohol, sex, hoarding, shopping, food – you name it. And as you probably know, the first step to overcoming any addiction is to give up the denial, the self-deceit. Because when a person begins to view themselves and their actions and consequences honestly, that's the first step of change. Only once they admit that there's a problem is it possible for them to see a way – an authentic way of living, and then they can start the healing that's required to grow.

See, letting go can be as much a part of honesty as forthcoming because honesty is a systematic examination of, and embracing of the truth. In developing honesty within yourself, you can become aware of who you truly are – the one you are when nobody is looking. It's being willing to be open, transparent, and vulnerable and live from that place, and to be straightforward and truthful with yourself when you aren't living up to your own standard of integrity that you've set for yourself.

We must be honest and value honesty with ourselves before we can be honest with others and before we can begin to identify our true intentions and goals. Honesty allows you to be authentic. It requires the courage and the willingness to look at yourself and not pull any punches in terms of who it is you are, and who it is you need to be, in order to do what it is that you want in your life.

Once we've taken this first step, often the hardest step towards self-honesty, we can then begin to take the other necessary steps to move forward toward our goals and toward being honest with others. The quickest way to develop impeccable honesty with others is to always keep your word. It sounds so simple, doesn't it? Yet all around us, lies are being told, and lies are being lived into in every aspect of our life: in our political figures, business leaders, athletes, entertainers, and sadly even in our religious organizations. And in each instance, there's a price to be paid beyond just the individuals involved.

In the Holy Bible, the Apostle Paul charged Timothy that first of all, prayers and giving of thanks be made for all men, that we may lead a quiet and peaceable life in all godliness and honesty. See, he considered it the highest of goals to live an honest life. Now, we've all seen the contrast of lives not lived honestly, and they are far from godly or peaceable. The trademark of a life lived without honesty is an unsettled, unsatisfied, frantic existence. So much energy goes into maintaining the fabricated persona that it truly does drain one's spirit.

And while there are dishonest people who appear to be quite prosperous, they will never experience the peace or unstoppable force of impeccable character. If you want to be effective in creating the life you envision and deserve, you will inevitably have to work with other people. Living and speaking from a place of impeccable honesty will gain you the respect and admiration needed to influence others. In short, consider this. The result that you and I experience in our lives is in direct proportion to the honesty which others perceive in us.

Something I have found helpful as a tool has been to ask myself these three questions regularly when communicating with others.

1. "Did I fully and honestly communicate what I really needed to say?"
2. "Did I hold back in any way? If so, was there something that I could have said to address my points more honestly?"
3. "Was I so preoccupied with how the other person might react that I edited my communication to something that was less than honest?"

You know, we all want to make sure that we're friendly and tactful when we express ourselves, but we need to be authentically honest without giving offense. I have found that honesty comes in three progressive stages. It begins with honesty within yourself. It then continues with honesty with others and then, by extension, honesty with your intentions and your actions. When what you say and do correlates with what you think and who you are at your core, it is said that you are congruent or in alignment; that you are living, being, and doing on the outside in a way that's matching what's happening on the inside. In other words, you must do what you said you would do in the way that you said you would do it.

When I'm examining how congruent I am in my words, thoughts, intentions, and actions, I ask myself some questions:

- Are my actions in alignment with and do they follow what I've stated my intentions to be?
- Am I acting in the most effective way possible to achieve those intentions?
- Am I resisting what needs to be done? Because if I'm resisting, I want to ask myself, why am I resisting?
- Is there incongruence between what needs to be done and my beliefs, values, or aspirations?
- Am I being fully honest with myself in regards to my intentions and my goals and my visions?

My mentor, Paul Martinelli, shared something he learned early in his personal development. It was one of those tough lessons that required a 'check-up from the neck up.' At one point his mentor said to him, "Paul, if you weren't living exactly the life you like, then be open to consider that maybe you're living your life less than honestly." Think about that. He said, "Be open to the consideration that if you're not living the life exactly as you want, that maybe you're living a life that's less than honest."

And, of course, he wasn't really happy about that idea. He wasn't intentionally living his life dishonestly, but had to remember what he said – the words, "Be open to the consideration." And he was. He spent several weeks considering the point. There was one other point his mentor shared, which was even more powerful. He said, "After you've considered that, that's the moment, right then, that you can start a completely new life journey. You can begin to live your life at a completely different level."

See, you will soon notice, as I did, that the ongoing practice of honesty in all aspects of our lives will transform us to the core. When we stay in our comfort zones, when we don't fully acknowledge our real hopes, our real dreams, when we just settle, and we become afraid to claim all the good that we really want in our lives, well, we're being dishonest with ourselves, and that's exactly what I was doing. I wanted much more, but I doubted my ability; I doubted my worldliness to have what it is that I wanted, and I purposely avoided being honest with my desires so I didn't have to face my fears and my doubts head on.

Motivational Speaker Les Brown, once said, "At times we are as honest as we can afford to be and as dishonest as we have to be with ourselves." I can't think of a simpler way to express it. What he also meant by that is - it's not just with ourselves, but in the relationships we've created, in which we know we cannot afford to be honest, whether we fear judgment or punishment or something else. Either way, internally, or in our relationships, if we allow the dishonesty to have control, if we shortchange ourselves, we rob ourselves of the feedback that we need to take corrective action. Without that feedback, we cannot grow to the next level; we stagnate in those toxic situations.

Imagine looking back at your life three years from today, knowing that you've lived a life of impeccable honesty with yourself, with others, with your hopes and your dreams. What would that life look like? Imagine it now as a life in which you've manifested your deepest, truest, honest self – your true desires; that you've accomplished the things that really matter to you; that you've developed the strong, resilient, unbreakable bonds and relationships.

See, as a daily practice, gauge your levels of openness with yourself, with others, and with your hopes, your dreams, your intentions, and your actions throughout the day and see how your practice of honesty can be deepened. This practice alone will give you access to greater power and resources than you ever thought possible. I'm confident that once you begin to experiment with this strategy, you will see how much more awaits undeveloped inside you, and you'll be energized to grow your life even more.

Honesty

NOTES

Vision

When I first started to become aware of creating a vision in 1998, I had decided to go back to school to get a degree in Nursing. I knew I had to do something to take care of me and my children because I didn't have the security of two paychecks. The divorce was hard on everyone but I was determined to make things "okay" for my kids. That's when I had the vision of a new life and a new journey as a Registered Nurse.

As I began to understand this idea, this strategy of vision, I realized I didn't just want financial prosperity, I wanted to be a better role model for my kids. I wanted a healthy lifestyle. I wanted to have a connection with God that was missing in my life for a number of years. My vision for our life together went much deeper than any paycheck I could receive.

A vision is something that emerges from our soul. A vision starts to take form and shape when you begin to see a life beyond your current conditions and circumstances; when you begin to identify your talents and resources hiding just below your consciousness. You begin to act with an informed or knowledgeable purpose, and the vision provides the highest guiding light for your emerging future.

Once I started to find ways to bring order to my thinking, order to my decision-making, I began to become aware of not only what some of my goals were, but I became crystal clear on who I was and what I was here to do - my purpose. I've heard John Maxwell say that the two most important days of our lives are the day that we were born and the day we find out why.

One of our country's most compelling examples of vision was expressed in President Kennedy's charge to NASA that the United States get to the moon by the end of the 1960s decade. During a speech in 1961 to Congress, he said that nothing will be more impressive to mankind, and none will be so difficult or expensive to accomplish. He went on to say that we aspire to do these things not because they are easy, but because they are hard. His vision for the nation was specific; it was clear; and it was delivered with passion and faith that comes with vision.

It was not a pipedream or a wish where people didn't really expect the plan to be fully acted out. See, instead, it was already fully envisioned and embraced by NASA's employees, from its top-level administrators all the way down to its janitorial staff. They understood the vision; they understood their responsibility in achieving the vision, even though they had no idea of how they were going to do it.

And that's where many of us, I think, get bogged down, isn't it? I know for me, in my own life, I tend to be a little bit left-brained, and I often get caught up on, "How am I going to do that?" In fact, we are naturally taught to consider the how first. We allow those voices from our past – right? – Our parents, teachers, employers, other people – to temper our aspirations with their self-doubt, with their skepticism, with their cynicism, with maybe even their negative self-judgment. We become conditioned not to get our hopes up, to self-censor our visions before they ever even rise fully into our conscious awareness.

True vision has been written about for thousands of years, even in ancient times. We can go back to the Bible in Proverbs 29. The passage speaks of many different things, of being righteous, wise, being humble. Its 27 verses offer guidance on a well-lived life. And among them, in verse 18 is this nugget, "Where there is no vision, the people perish." You know, for years, when I read that, I thought it meant that literally people would physically die. Later, as I expanded my understanding through study, I realized, worse yet, they don't die; they live with a lack of awareness of their true, God-given potential.

Motivational Speaker Les Brown made an observation one time. He said that some people die at age 25 and don't get buried until they're 65. What he means is that, without vision, people genuinely have no future; that without vision, they are cast upon the junk heap of life. So, without vision, they become a liability to society rather than an asset to those around them. Without vision, their mentality is more about existing than truly living, and that is perishing. The verse assumes that there is a vision to be revealed in all of us. One has to have a purpose and promise. The vision of a revelation from God – G-O-D again, the Grand Overall Designer – makes a person walk a certain path.

Vision is a useful and powerful tool, in the learning model of success, to guide and direct us towards living a meaningful life. Vision allows us to connect with our purpose and become very clear of our goals. I've learned over time that identifying one's purpose at first can seem daunting. But don't worry. Your vision will help you identify it. Your vision is your way to attain the unattainable. It's your ability to reach God's consciousness, the ultimate presence that exists above and beyond our awareness, our conditions and our circumstances.

And as you'll hear me say many times during these strategies, your current circumstances – my current circumstances – will never be able to predict what you and I are capable of doing in our lives. The formulation, articulation, and application of a vision are an exercise truly of the law of cause and effect. The internal vision that we become aware of, that we co-create in our life, is the cause. And the external expression of that vision, which we define as results, is the effect. The results in our life will always be an expression of what we truly believe is possible in our life. And that belief in possibility begins with a fortified vision for our lives.

When there is a true vision or revelation of one's higher power or infinite spirit, what I call the voice of God within us, it has the power to motivate us, inspire us, but only if we have an awareness of it and reverence to conduct our lives in harmony with our highest good. People who live and operate without vision have a propensity to engage in self-destructive behavior, procrastination, and negativity. They act out of blindness. They will not discipline themselves to take proper responsibility, and the result is that they perish. Quite a contrast to the satisfying result a person experiences when they are living in and from their vision.

See, there can be no doubt what a vision produces. And the beautiful thing about vision is that you don't have to go searching for it; it's already within you. It's not as much about finding a vision as much as it is about discovering the vision that has been inside you all along. Its finer points will undoubtedly change and evolve over time, but if allowed, its foundation will bring order, focus, and cohesiveness to all aspects of your life.

Here's how. Vision is the conscious awareness of our desires and possibilities blended with the gift of imagination. Vision is our ability to create our future with passion today. But vision is just not a destination; it's also a powerful tool that allows us to engage all of our senses, our resources, and emotions into this realization.

So, vision not only yields a mental picture of our future result, but also a mental construction of the sights, sounds, feeling, emotions, or vibrations and frequencies. It sets up the vibration or frequency of expectation for success, as the mind works through the problems and positive vibrations and frequencies are imprinted and extended out to the universe.

Athletes often use their vision to improve their performance. We'll see an Olympic skier, for example, will close their eyes and quite literally see the vision of a run down the mountain. She can see and feel her performance, the cuts, the leans, and the wind blowing by. And she begins to engage all the muscles as though she was actually making each turn on the run. And she sees the outcome. She actually feels the exhilaration of the wind. You see, experience through imagination is experience nonetheless.

So, in the context of the strategies, the internal aspect of your vision is who you become. The external aspect of your vision is what you create and achieve. Your internal vision is the mental model of perfection that you co-create in your life. This is living into your full potential in your most productive and fulfilling venture. It is the image of the person you would be beyond your limiting self-beliefs, your fears, doubts, self-judgments. It is the true, powerful, compassionate, creative, caring, resource-filled driven person that you are when you are completely present at your fullest potential.

Your external vision is the expression and manifestation of your internal vision. In essence, it's the results that you get in every area of your life. This includes results that you've realized in your relationships, in your spiritual growth, in the health of your physical body, in what you create in terms of your financial and material wealth.

This is the beauty of transformation. The path of vision in the strategies allows you to transform internally, and thereby alter your external results, creating the change you desire in your life.

You know, if you're like most people, thinking about and visualizing the external is scary, right? Our goals and our dreams may be more attractive at first, but soon you'll begin to realize that the real benefit of holding and living from your vision is actually internal. It's about who you become. If your vision is purely external – in other words, if you focus exclusively on outward achievement, the getting of physical results, you will never grow to be the person who can create and manifest these things internally in your life.

We want to be very intensive, very vigilant of our inner world. Your vision allows you to be who you want to become in your thoughts, in your character, in your beliefs, in your awareness, and in your actions. So, never lose sight of your true limitless core. In my mentoring and coaching program, one of the exercises I share with my students, to crystallize their internal vision, is to write out a vision statement. So, I would encourage you to do the same right here. And I'll share with you some of the things that you may want to consider as you write out your statement.

I had read a lot of books on goal achieving but it wasn't until I read a statement from Eric Hoffer did I understand what I needed to learn. He said, "In order for us to learn anything, it requires two degrees of confidence. First, if we have too little confidence, we think we cannot learn. And second, if we have too much confidence, worse yet, we think we don't have to."

So, as I share this exercise, don't let the simplicity of what I'm sharing with you derail you from actually doing the exercise. This is the exercise. This is the process of really living in and from this strategy of vision.

So, number one is you want to write out your vision in present tense, as though it's already been completed. For example, if we're writing, "One day I will have a house of my dreams," we want to write that, "Right now I'm living in the house of my dreams." We're going to change that from what I will have to what I am now living in present tense.

Second, we want to be very specific. After all, if you're the architect of your dream and your future, what does that house look like? What does it literally look like? How large is it? Where is it located? How many bedrooms does it have?

Number three is we want to become emotionally involved in the vision that you've created. How does living in this home allow you to feel? How would you be feeling to live the lifestyle of that home? What would your emotional state be? Defining your emotional state allows you to create the vibration of expectation that I talked about earlier

Number four, why don't you take some time to identify the people that you want in your life? Who would be with you on this journey? If you're living that which is trying to emerge from your soul, who would be the people in your life?

Number five, what beliefs and values would you be holding and living from if you were fully present in this vision? Chances are some of the things that you believe now will have to change in order for this vision to be realized in your life. Some of the things that you value now may become less important, and you will develop a new set of values. Other values may become more solidified. What does this new set of beliefs and values look like?

Think of this as a journal entry about your actions and note your feelings and the sights and sounds that surround you. This exercise can help you further define and clarify your purpose and goals by creating an emotional impact and attachment and positive vibration regarding your vision. Just as the Olympic skier is able to mentally meet her goal of success before it becomes a physical reality, as she flies down the mountain, the vibration of expectation that you create will allow you to fashion the specific goals to make your vision a successful reality. You are then making real progress towards your life's purpose.

The vision that you create for yourself, and over the years you'll have many, must be clear that you bring it into your consciousness easily, like Kennedy's vision of reaching the moon. Vision serves as the connector between your life's purpose and the goals you will set to realize it. As you continue, you will see how all the strategies will provide an awareness of all of your own resources, strategies, and tactics to further strengthen your vision, life's purpose, and resolve.

I ask you, even if you're a little bit skeptical, to remain open to this potential reality of the limitless you and read the remaining strategies from this open-minded state. Be very present. See, if you sense that spark, if you feel the possibility awakening inside you, know that you have all the resources necessary to support you on your journey. I invite you, if you would like some help on this journey, to join me in one of my coaching programs. You can take part in the step-by-step program or be part of a group of committed people who are willing to give you support, hold you accountable, and help you clarify your vision. I'm totally confident you will fulfill your vision.

NOTES

Persistence

Persistence is the quality of continuing to be in the action of doing, in moving forward despite the problems, difficulties or hardships that have come along the way. In other words, persistence is taking us all the way to our final achievement.

You know, we live in a culture that expects instant gratification, and where many people have developed a sense of entitlement. We expect movies on demand, 24-hour customer service; we want fast food; basically, we want everything pretty easy in our lives. We see this in our over-budgeted and debt-ridden households, where many young people believe that they should be rewarded – not because of their achievements, but simply because they tried or, worse yet, simply because they just showed up.

You know if you're like most people, just hearing the word persistence brings about a sensation or image of struggle, of unending effort or challenge that has to be endured. Well, in the context of the strategies, persistence is seen from a far more positive and optimistic view. It's not about enduring. In fact, it's far from it. Instead, persistence is about actively doing whatever must be done with purpose, passion, and inspiration. This type of persistence does not have an end. Its core is where you develop your daily motivation to live your vision, whether it's minute by minute, hour by hour, or day by day.

Colin Powell was recognized as saying "Success is the result of perfection, hard work, learning from failure, loyalty, and persistence." See, what Colin Powell was trying to say here is that just because you show up for work on time, update your knowledge, do what you said you will do, and finish what you start, while all of this may not be glamorous or make for interesting conversation, it will, however, define the basic building blocks of success in all aspects of life, even beyond such traditional measures such as natural ability, developed talent, or education. Most people – 85 percent of people – after the first or second failure, defeat, or disappointment, they quit. They don't learn from their failures. They aren't willing to do what the great Og Mandino said, "Persist until you succeed."

There is a Japanese proverb that says, "Fall seven times; stand up eight." I love that. Persistence carries the tenacity, the intensity, the fire and the relentless passion that naturally arise when you are living in alignment with your heart's desire. It means that we keep trying even when we fail, because we know we're learning and growing in competence with each failed attempt. And as such, we're getting closer to our success and a new level of awareness that will ultimately carry us forward. This process makes all the difference in our journey. Without persistence, the other strategies cannot be engaged, and they lose their transformational power. With it, however, your life can be changed forever.

Persistence is closely tied with resolution. You resolve to act in alignment with your vision. Often, our daily routines and personal interactions can weigh us down as burdens, or we can choose to fuel our actions with passionate resolution and intensity, in which case they can lift us and provide us motivation to persistently move forward towards fulfilling our vision. This is the way of the strategies. Even necessary, mundane actions will burn with fire and passion and heat so the journey becomes enjoyable, just as the destination will be.

You know, inevitably in life, we face situations and tasks that we would rather not have to face. There's a saying that's appropriate, "Nobody trips over mountains." Most times, it's the small pebbles that cause us to stumble. As we pass all the small pebbles on our path, we soon we find that we've crossed a mountain.

The first phase of developing any habit requires determination. It takes a huge amount of energy or effort versus a lot of time. Lots of people give up because they realize the level of energy or effort it's going to take, and they decide, "This isn't meant to be – I'll try something else." At the peak of that effort, though, the amount of time starts to level off, and as we are able to reproduce the action, we enter the next phase which requires persistence or sticking with it. Now, you have to keep doing the thing over and over and over again, and that's where people give up, because it feels like it's going to take forever.

Here's an example. I recently changed the location of the scissors in my kitchen. And after a month, I still found myself going to the drawer to get the scissors when they were right in front of me in the new holder on the counter. Old habits die hard. You see, the final phase is when the energy and effort start dropping off quickly, and it now becomes a habit. There's no more effort over time, but it requires patience. What happens is our old behavior will suddenly resurface. We must be persistent and not allow that to happen. Persistence is the ability to reproduce that success over and over and over again, through to completion.

In your personal journey, you will have to face situations, confront people or change internal habits. Whether you want to build a high rise or lose weight, both are filled with challenges, friction, internal and external opposition, and the momentum that's going to have to be changed. Yet in either case, when we live embedded in persistence, our inner fire burns brighter than any challenge that has to be overcome. In fact, when we truly embody the concept of persistence, in its most essential and true manifestation, we look forward to and embrace the challenges. We will seek them out. The fire within us burns so strong that we can overcome the pebbles on our path, and no matter the size of the obstacle, it just adds fuel to the fire so that our resolution and intensity grow to match it.

Have you seen the best athletes at the top of their game, when the stakes are raised, and their intensity increases? We've all heard the saying, "Rise to the challenge." Through weeks and months and sometimes years of training, the athlete develops the habit of persistence in which they now sharpen their resolution to face any obstacle. It inspires the bystanders, the spectators, and it touches internally every one of us in a very fundamental way.

Persistence is not concerned with action per se. It's not just about trying your best; it's about taking it all the way to accomplishment. Persistence says, "If you have ever tried your best, and you haven't accomplished your goal, then get better."

Persistence is continuously doing things necessary to not only get better but to reach the goal. You see, persistence is concerned with accomplishment, with results, and it carries a time component. Your effort will have order, structure, and direction brought about through your vision and your focus.

Without vision and focus to structure your efforts, your actions would likely mirror those of people whose lives are filled with action but no real accomplishment. They wake up; they cook; they eat; they fill their day with errands from their to-do list, but get absolutely nowhere. They're busy, but they're not productive. This type of activity has nothing to do with persistence; it's only about keeping the mind and body occupied.

Remember, persistence is a strategy only concerned with accomplishment. So, even though you've persisted, if you didn't accomplish your goal, then it's time to be persistent about getting better so you can. After all, you're trying to achieve a much broader vision here for your life. Persistence is a commitment to the end result. In the process of commitment to the end result, persistence will have you sharpen your skills and advance your learning in every area of your life.

There is a book called Think and Grow Rich by Napoleon Hill that should be a part of everyone's library. In the chapter on persistence, he says that persistence is a state of mind; therefore, it can be cultivated. He said, "Like all states of mind, persistence is based upon definite causes," and he lists what he calls his eight factors of persistence. The first one is definiteness of purpose; the second is desire; the third is self-reliance; the fourth definiteness of plans; the fifth is accurate knowledge; the sixth, co-operation; the seventh is willpower; and the eighth is habit.

If you haven't had a chance to read Think and Grow Rich yet, or if you haven't read it in the last 12 months, I encourage you to pick the book up and dive in, especially in the chapter on persistence.

If I hadn't been persistent in pursuing my dreams of helping people, you wouldn't be reading this now.

Before we move to the next strategy, let me share this with you: your habits are what define your hours, your days, and your life. Your habits will define how you persist towards your final goals and your achievements. Remember that persistence is not a burden - but a blessing. Hold on and keep going. Stick to your vision, be persistent, and soon it will be realized.

NOTES

Focus

You know, we live in a wondrous world full of sights, sounds, and motions. But amidst all of these stimuli, it is really easy for us to be distracted from what is really important to us.

There are several definitions of focus that could be helpful as we start to engage in this topic. Focus is an act of concentrating on our interests, energy, attention, or activity. It means to converge on, or toward, a central point, or to bring ideas or emotions into alignment. It can also convey maximum clarity or distinctness of image.

Just as vision helps define our life's purpose and identify objectives to help us reach it, focus gives us clarity and concentrates our energy and activity to help us reach and grab our goals, in order to carry out our life's purpose. But, in truth, in today's fast-paced society, focus is becoming scarcer in our lives than ever before. Part of our distraction lies in the overwhelming number of choices we are asked to make each day.

For instance, I was recently at Starbucks (I'm a big Starbucks fan.) Now there are times I like a specialty coffee, but this particular day I was thinking quick and easy – in and out. In looking at the menu the decisions I had to make to buy a simple cup of coffee were staggering. Did I want it tall, grande, or venti? Did I want it bold, medium or mild in flavor? Did I want it skinny or sweet with sugar or honey? What about whip? It was never-ending. I just wanted a large cup of coffee with cream and sugar but it was hard to focus – hard to find how to order that particular cup. Have you experienced this?

Even the simple task of buying toothpaste can be far more complex than it was just only a decade ago. Do you know that currently there are 41 different kinds of Crest toothpaste? Couple this with the overwhelming number of consumer choices with our never-ending addiction to technology and ways information is accessed through laptops, iPods, iPads, iPhones, TV cable channels, and the complexity of just modern living multiplies many-times over.

We rush from meetings to activities, fitting in quick meals and even quicker actual conversations with one another while constantly surrounding ourselves with sights, sounds, and stimuli of all kinds. Although silence may be golden, today it is rarely heard.

What about the fact that we average three televisions per home, with only 2.5 people per home? Think about it. How many televisions are in your house? What about phones or computers, or just gadgets that you take around with you on a regular basis? As a speaker and trainer, I travel all over the world. This is not just something here in the United States; it is the same everywhere.

Have you ever sat and watched a teenager? They will usually have three or four forms of technology in front of them at one time: a TV, a computer, and a cell phone that they are texting on – all while listening to their iPod. They appear to be masters of multitasking, and our society has come to expect it from us. Even then, we purchase more and more gadgets so we can be connected to information 24 hours a day, 7 days a week, with no downtime.

Don't get me wrong: I have an iPhone. Those of you who know me, I use email and the phone a lot. I love it because it allows me to connect with, and help, people all over the world. When I connect with my clients,

I don't multitask. However, I know that many people do operate that way, and it is easy to do it. You may be one of them. In our effort to be more productive, we try to do more things in less time. But in reality, I believe it is to our own detriment. We only need to look at the airline incident where distracted pilots overshot their city by 100 miles before they realized they even missed it or the tragic consequences of our youth texting while they drive.

On one of her shows, Oprah devoted an entire show to the growing number of deaths in auto accidents attributed to cell phone use. One of her guests – a University of Utah professor who studied distracted drivers for ten years – talked about the research that showed our brains literally cannot process peripheral visual cues when we drive and talk on the phone. His study showed that when our brains are focusing to process a phone conversation while our bodies are physically engaged to drive the car that our mind sees only what is directly ahead of us. It cannot process the peripheral cues of the elderly person on the sidewalk about to step into the street, or the kid on the bike to the left just barely out of our vision. That is why many states have passed laws against using cell phones while driving. I predict in some cities we are going to begin to see laws against texting, emailing, or instant messaging even while we are walking on our city streets.

Motivational Speaker Les Brown points out while focus is proven mandatory, it is one of the most difficult things we can do today. This is critical for us to realize, for much of goal achievement lies in the realm of creativity, and creating is a completely separate process from consuming and communicating information. Therefore, it is especially difficult to create when our energy is diffused in multiple directions at once. Under these conditions, if you can access your creative process at all, it is considerably slowed. It is safe to say that multitasking diminishes our creative effectiveness.

To better understand the significance seemingly small distractions can make, think about the distraction of a small canopy of shade. This interruption of the sun's rays can deflect our world's most powerful energy source to create a cool space amidst a hot surrounding. In contrast, a typical laser is a very low-energy source of light, but because of its pinpoint focus, it can be harnessed to penetrate almost any material.

Focus is precision energy. Most of us think that focus is about tuning out the distractions. After all, we know that distractions are a part of life; we don't have perfect control of our environment. But there is another proactive way to think about how we accept our reality. I invite you to consider what I teach to coaching students that focus is also tuning into the right positive influences, a thoughtful control of what we let into our minds.

On what specifically should you begin to focus to increase the power in your life? When I am working with someone in a coaching situation, I like to ask my clients these four seemingly simple questions.

1. What are you absolutely great at?
2. What skills do you possess that others admire in you?
3. Are these things that you love to do?
4. Can you have a meaningful income from them?

Four simple questions with perhaps just one or two ready answers right now, but soon they help you identify the activities you value more, the activities worthy of your focus, worthy of your time, your energy, and your activity.

Ancient Buddhists wrote that a focused mind is more powerful than a thousand elephants. I think a thousand may be too few for this saying, for really there is no limit to what we can produce with our mind. By mastering the art of focus, you will learn to harness that power, concentrating your body's activity and your spirit's vision into a singular intention with specific results.

You can learn to tap the full force of your being and guide it to carry out and fulfill your life's purpose. It is so easy to underestimate the difficulty of becoming focused. In concept, it is quite simple, but it is a lot more difficult than it sounds. Many well-intended people set out to be focused fully aware of its importance, but find themselves in frustration when they fall into one of the distractions of life, and let's face it, there's many of those distraction traps.

You see, our goals consist of both glamorous and mundane elements. It is easy to get caught up in the excitement of all the opportunities and possibilities associated with a project or a goal only to let some of the routine, but critical obligations, fall into neglect.

What would any ideal day of focus on each separate activity look like for you? For me it would be a day in which every moment has a perfect intention that you've determined with foresight. When you are focused, each moment you spend moves you closer to your desired outcome. I say "spend," not "invest," because time is precious, but perishable. Time does not give dividends or refunds. When it's gone, it's gone. What survives? What survive are the results you've achieved and the consequences of your thoughts, words, and actions.

Every moment that goes by is a point in the continuum of life. The quality of your life will be in direct proportion to your ability to focus.

People can execute routine obligations in a low state of focus, almost on autopilot. Many people go about their days without full awareness of what the moment brings and takes away. Few understand the many ways they can respond to any one moment, and how their response makes an impact on the next moment, and the next, and the next.

As with each strategy, focus has two main components that if you are able to master them will change your life forever. The first focus component is your ability to deliberately concentrate on a specific subject. In fact, the very word "concentrate" denotes power, doesn't it? If we think of concentrated detergent or juice concentrate, it's extremely potent. You have to be disciplined enough and committed enough that you aren't going to allow anything to intervene or interfere with whatever it is you are trying to do.

The strength of your commitment allows you to maximize potential and be able to extract out that which you want to achieve while you focus on your goals. That level of concentration, or focus, takes you into a zone of achievement, performance, and mastery that most people never achieve because most people focus on the distractions rather than their destiny.

The second focus component concerns your ability to be knowledgeable about what you have focused on. Almost anything has value if we make the effort to concentrate on it and look beneath the surface to explore its depth below.

I live close to the beach in Florida. For those of you who have viewed the ocean in person from any distance, the ocean looks much the same to many people looking at it from a long view or an overview. We see the surface, and maybe we catch some glimpses of what is beneath. But, if you put on a snorkel and mask, then you open up your eyes and your view and your focus to a whole new world. If you study it and look beneath, a diverse and vibrant new world exists. It would not be possible to fully focus on each action, each movement, each creature, each plant or nuance of the water's movement.

Life is too short to focus on everything, for to do so you would be focusing, really, on nothing. Therefore, your focus must be aligned with your vision and your life's purpose. Think of it this way. If you believe that at this very moment, as you're hearing my voice, that you are going to discover a way to give special value to every moment that follows, that what I was going to say was going to change your life forever, then I am sure that you would pay your closest possible attention. This is purposeful focus: a literal visual representation, or manifestation, of where you are and where you are going. It is your ability to be fully present, with the added bonus that you have a clear purpose for the outcome of this moment. A mind that is brought to a single, pointed awareness is far more powerful at accomplishing anything that it is set upon. If you are hearing this with perfect focus, you would have a predetermined intention for what you are going to get out of this moment.

Have you ever wanted to learn something new but figured it was too hard to even try? Perhaps you didn't believe in the possibility you could do it because someone told you it wasn't possible? I want you to know it's very possible. When we allow purpose and focus to be blended with the predetermined intention, we have possibility. It is this simple, almost insignificant distinction which brings about a powerful transformation in our lives.

I have found that one of the distinctions between ordinary results and extraordinary results is simple: The focused person has a predetermined inner agreement that he or she will get something valuable out of every moment, and whatever he or she learns will be put into practice. By contrast, a person who has out-of-focus results engages in short bursts of mental entertainment and then gets distracted by whatever impulse catches their attention – whether it is email, a coffee break, or a text message from a friend.

Focus will allow you to conserve energy, time, and resources by harnessing your power to follow the critical path to success. Emerson said this, "Where your focus goes, your energy flows." If your focus is in a thousand different directions, then your energy is scattered, weakened, and disorganized. Your focus on these strategies is a positive step toward directing your energy and concentrating its power on what really matters to you: which should be living your life's purpose.

NOTES

Courage

Here is a great quote that I absolutely love. It says, "Life is not about waiting for the storms to pass. It is about learning how to dance in the rain." I like it because it reflects the purpose-driven courage that we need to achieve our vision and fulfill our life's purpose regardless of our circumstances. The word "courage" is actually derived from the old French word, courage, whose Latin origin, cor, means heart and spirit. It resides within, and although most of our study of courage comes from historical and political figures, there is abundance of courage in everyday life that we should recognize and appreciate. These would include people who stand up for their principles or values, volunteer for the difficult assignment at work, or start a new business in their neighborhood.

All major accomplishments that we see were daring at first. It took courage to stand against the popular opinion of the majority and say, "Here I stand for I can do no other." Anything of consequence – politically or economically – any major transformation in governments, corporations, big decisions that went against popular opinion required this concept of courage.

In our own lives, long-term personal transformation also requires the courage to face our fears, anxieties, and to move ahead outside of our comfort zone and our safety net. It is often easier to understand courage in the political and physical realm of our lives, but we also need to be aware of how courage exists primarily in the realm of our morals, in our motions and our personal actions.

Courage is an essential strategy for living the life you deserve. It really isn't optional. Although most dictionaries list bravery as a synonym of courage, I believe that there is a difference. I once heard someone describe it like this: Bravery is for those who conquer someone or something else; courage is for those who conquer their own fears. I like that distinction. We can witness bravery in the extraordinary actions of firefighters and emergency medical personnel. Certainly, our police officers exhibit such acts of bravery every day.

But courage is not about overcoming the external forces that act upon others, but the internal forces that we act upon ourselves. Therefore, our strategy definition of courage is about the quality of mind or spirit that enables a person to face difficulty, danger, pain, and other changes, including their ability to do what must be done in spite of their internal resistance of fear.

In this light, courage has little to do with a macho mindset, and everything to do with humbleness of spirit. It involves tapping into the valor and core strength needed when you are committed to following your vision and life purpose, believing that it comes from your higher power. Confucius said, "To see what is right and not to do- it is want of courage." Trusting your source of power will provide you with the humble, yet steadfast courage to do the right thing.

Just as courage is different from bravery, it is also different from confidence. No matter how much confidence a person has, it still requires courage to act. Confidence can help get you started on your vision, but it is courage that will see you all the way through. We can take heart, however, that as with the other strategies, courage can be developed. We can start by anticipating the obstacles that we will face and by creating the fortitude within ourselves to overcome them. In fact, the greatest obstacle we will face is also our greatest master teacher. It is our own fear, and it is the fertile soil upon which we can sow courage.

No one has ever developed courage by avoiding fear or avoiding unpleasant circumstances. Therefore, if you want to become courageous, you cannot avoid situations that trigger your fears – whether they are physical or mental.

Of course, we don't go looking for fear, right? It comes to us. If one thing is certain, it is that the path leading to your vision, your goals, your life's purpose, are going to be filled with moments and experiences that will trigger and awaken your greatest fears. Courage becomes, really, the willingness to act in spite of your fears and reservations.

You may think fear is always going to be a major player in your life. But we can make it a minor player by the willingness to feel the courage and act in spite of the fear. This is where, really, all of our growth comes from.

If we allow ourselves to surrender to fear, then we allow the circumstances and fear to master our lives and we are living a fear-driven life. If we live in spite of our fears, then we are living a faith-driven life, which allows us to be willing to risk failure and disappointment or fall on our face and make some big mistakes.

I read something once that Fred Smith, the CEO of FedEx wrote. He said, "If you haven't made any major mistakes in your life by age 35, then you haven't done anything with your life." I think that most people allow fear of failure and defeat to hold them back because that is the way our educational system has really conditioned us. Failure is punishment, and daring and risk-taking really is discouraged.

Courage allows you to make it okay to live beyond the good opinions of others. It allows you to be willing to lay it all on the line. The critical point to master is that you face the fear on the road to your vision. Make no mistake; you will always encounter fears in your life. Whether you wander aimlessly or move in the direction of your vision, you are going to face fear. One path takes you nowhere. The other will transform your life.

Let's look at some of the ways that fear shows up. Boy, can't we count the ways. I think one of the biggest is procrastination. Procrastination is one of fear's allies – putting things off, being too busy, and not being willing to take on any new task.

The dishonesty that arises from not being authentic to your true values or from being unwilling to express what you need is another form of fear. Indeed, courage is to honesty what carbon is to steel. Honesty is built upon the foundation of courage. In the absence of courage, honesty will falter.

Fear lurks closer than just our own shadow. Unfortunately, we have the ability to avoid it, ignore it, and continue our life under a subtle yet uneasy pretense that fear is held at bay. Rather than live with this pretense, you must be prepared to face the fears that will inevitably come if you want to move forward in your life.

One way to develop the fortitude to face your fear is by doing what you are doing right now. Through study, learning, and understanding we can expand our awareness of our potential and create knowledge of a higher truth than the limiting beliefs that our fears are based on. In effect, we are creating courage through understanding.

We know that ignorance breeds fear. We are uncomfortable and afraid of things or people of which we are unfamiliar with or that we don't understand. Studying and learning the strategies will help fortify your courage through your increased awareness and understanding.

Listen, everyone has fears. Your fears may have developed from a past experience, especially if it was one of those where someone with power or authority over you has said some negative things about your performance or about your future. Your willingness to stand your ground and take the heat and pressure is the essence of courage. We all have the capacity to do that, but a majority of people are followers, thermometers that reach to the outside temperature. We need to be the thermostat that sets the temperature. We need to raise the bar, operate from the thinking that Henry David Thoreau said, "Don't go where the path may lead; go where there is no path and leave a trail." It is about leaving a trail. It is about creating a new path, a new vision for your life.

I personally believe that risk, or calculated courage, is an essential element to success. I don't know of any successful person who does not take calculated risks. Courage and risk-taking is not only necessary for achieving success; it is necessary for sustaining success. Courage allows you to act in the face of doubts and fears. It is the ability to go into any situation and show up authentically, express yourself from your heart, and allow yourself to show up joyfully in full self-expression.

Do not be timid as you think of a goal right now that will move you towards your vision – something you must work for but that you really want. Now, resolve to get it. Taking the first action and direction of this goal is as simple as taking a moment to write it down. I encourage you to do that now. Write down your goal – something you really want, something which is realistic at this point in your journey, something that you must strive for to achieve. As you write it, say it aloud, "I want," and you fill in the blank of your life. What do you really want, is it something you want that will move you toward your internal and external vision at this point of your life? Just commit to taking the next action step towards reaching your goal.

I am absolutely convinced that in any goal-achievement process, everybody knows at least what their next step is. Even if that next step isn't monumental, even if that next step isn't going to lead to a quantum leap, it is still what you need to do to get there eventually. Write that action down by completing the following sentence: My first action toward reaching my goal will be – and then you fill in the blank of your life. What is your first action going to be?

As you think about your first action step, do you notice any discomfort or maybe resistance arising in you? Can you see how immediately, even subtly, fear can appear? You may resist taking your action step not because you're too busy, not because you have other things to do, not because you know you can take care of it at another time; you may resist it because of fear. Maybe fear has crept into your present reality, and you know you won't be able to take this action, even if it leads you towards something you really want.

Many times, when I was looking at these exercises as a student while on my journey, on my path, I never filled in the blanks. That was my way of procrastination. That's how my fear manifested.

If you haven't taken the time to do this, I encourage you to do it now. What is a goal that you really want, and what will be your first action step?

As you continue to grow your courage, remember that few things worthwhile in life are easy, and it is the discomfort that causes us to grow. The words "growing pains" really are true. You are going to face countless situations that will stir your fear. You will recognize them because they will make you uncomfortable and cause you to procrastinate or be dishonest with yourself, with others, or with your intentions.

Observe yourself reacting to the fear that comes, but distance yourself from its emotions. Simply take note of the feelings when they arise and what precipitated them. Was it a new opportunity? Was it a challenge, a difficulty, maybe a conflict? Maybe it is a risk you need to take. Identify your fears the moment they arise.

I love what my friend and mentor, John Maxwell says. He says, "Shovel while the pile is small." Begin to consciously take note of the circumstances that sparked fear in you. This will give you insights into your own resistance, which you can then begin to honestly explore. Returning, then, to the second strategy of honesty can help you build this level of self-awareness.

We want to be very vigilant regarding the internal state that we're in. As you begin to waver in facing challenges, hold true to your core. Draw upon the vast resources of your being, of your vision, of you and the life that you have always longed for.

A well-known author, photographer, and Buddhist monk, Matthieu Ricard, wrote it this way; he said: "It's not the magnitude of the task that matters; it's the magnitude of our courage." So, be courageous as you go and grow forward. It will make all the difference in achieving success.

Courage

NOTES

Intuition

Hello and welcome. I'm Michele Sfakianos and in this lesson, I want to talk about strategy Number 7 – Intuition and the role intuition plays in a successful and rewarding life.

You know, our intuition is without question one of the most powerful resources available to us. When we use it correctly it can magnify the benefits we receive from applying all of the other Strategies. Intuition is something which I think we've all had experience with. I know intuition has made a significant difference in my life and in every area of my life. But I also know that although we can see its results, we often have a difficult time understanding where it comes from or how to apply it to achieving our broader vision in life's purpose.

Part of this confusion is in realizing that we're really dealing with two types of intuition. The late Wayne Dyer, a phenomenal teacher, said "If prayer is you talking to God then intuition is God talking to you." That's really the first type of intuition. It's spiritual intuition and it comes from a deep connection with God and the universe. It is a powerful way for us to understand the essence of our thoughts and our beliefs.

Our second type of intuition has more of a basis in experience or realistic knowledge. I've lost my keys and an hour later I've gotten a hunch where they are and that's exactly where I find them. You've probably had many similar experiences.

Today all of our lives are more complex than ever. By now in this strategy book we've become fully aware of how the world's distractions can divert us from achieving our vision and our life's purpose. For this reason alone, understanding and honing your intuition, both the spiritual and experiential type is essential for sound decision making.

As a strategy your intuitive faculty must be unleashed so that it can help illuminate your journey. The power of learning to trust your intuition will help you identify potential pitfalls before they can harm you or hold you back from achieving your full potential. It can also bring people into your life who can help unfold your vision and into your field of awareness - bring new opportunities.

Intuition allows you to see possibilities. It also helps you to effectively choose the options that will most quickly turn those possibilities into re-alities. I've worked with many people who want to develop their own in-tuitive abilities. One of the mistakes they make is feeling that they have to force their mind to do the work in a proactive way. Believing that they have to almost make it happen; but really true intuition is a neutral per-spective and it can be perceived only when we allow ourselves to just be and not by projecting our own agenda into the world.

Intuition is the ability to reference the subtle sensory information that we're gaining. What is outside our conscious perception? It is our knowledge without direct sensory experience. As a result, a direction al-ways proceeds from this true perspective. Learning to recognize and trust that voice from within may feel uncomfortable at first, simply because it is unfamiliar.

As you learn more about and embrace your intuitive capability you will realize that this is not hocus-pocus, or some new age mumbo jumbo. Intuition stems from your higher self and it has been made available to you for your life's benefit. Now to understand how to take advantage of the benefits of this strategy let's examine the two types: Experiential and spiritual intuition more closely. Experiential intuition stems from our collective life experiences and knowledge. The simplest way to understand this type of intuition is to think of it as learned recognition. Your subconscious mind over time develops connections between your new situation and events and experiences from your past. These connections are helpful for decision making, interpretation, and processing when faced with incomplete or imperfect information.

In psychology they call these hierarchies. The connections are like steps of a ladder which your brain has created as a helpful tool for you. You automatically access those steps to get the right answer in any given situation. It's likely you would not be able to articulate the elements of the connection nor the steps of the ladder, but they are, nevertheless very real. This type of intuition comes as an inner voice. But it is really a well thought out process of your subconscious to respond to a particular type of problem or a circumstance, and it is something that is meant to be accessed over and over again.

I think all of us have probably walked into a party or been to a business meeting or gathering and we can sense immediately when something isn't right in the situation or with another person. Using these areas of knowledge that we have sharpened over the years; we can perceive important cues without even consciously knowing why. These are imperceptible to most people. Some may concede that Simon Cowell of American Idol had experiential, intuitive skills regarding talent. So, he could make very quick decisions about people's potential success, even if he didn't always articulate his viewpoint in a very friendly way.

In the best-selling book Blink by Malcolm Gladwell there are a number of fascinating examples of adaptive subconscious or experiential intuition, like the insurance adjuster who can quickly identify a counterfeit statue. Or a woman who has an uncanny ability to identify a successful new cookie recipe, now, that's not a bad gig if you can get it right? But our subconscious mind over time develops these connections between your new situations, opportunities, events, and experiences of the past. These connections are helpful for decision making, interpretation, and processing when you are faced with incomplete or maybe even imperfect information.

You likely can't articulate the connections but they are very real nonetheless. The second and I believe more profound type of intuition involves practice. Not for gaining experiential knowledge but for gaining trust. It is a trust of your universal power. Trust in the power that I define as God. What others may call infinite intelligence spirit or creative power, it's an understanding, an awareness and trust in our connection to that power, and to all things through which we receive it.

This spiritual type of intuition is already part of your being, and it's the kind I spoke of earlier. Knowing who is calling before you look at the phone. Of learning of a far-away loved one just as the thought pops into your mind and you find out that they indeed do need you now. It's our power to tap into or resonate with any and all vibrations or frequencies in the universe. All of these small and profound inklings or hunches serve as proof that there is a quality within you that can be trusted.

It extends beyond your five physical senses, existing within the nuance vibration from others, no matter where they are in the universe. Like a muscle it too can be developed through the repetition of conscious and deliberate use. It's vital that you actively develop this power in your life for several reasons. First, it can give you an obvious advantage by acting as a short-cut in your decision making. Intuition provides an alternative source of power that offers you more information, more intelligence data by which you can make your decisions so you can make them more quickly and more importantly, with more confidence than ever before. Like Simon Cowell or the examples in Blink you will just know what's good. You'll just know what's right and true for all you have to do is trust that choice.

Secondly, intuition allows you to more fully experience your oneness with your higher power and the life's purpose that's yearning to be expressed through you. Like the musician through whom the words and music to a song pour out in minutes but goes on to touch millions over decades, this creative energy and truth lies beyond your logical knowing and the appearance of your conditions or circumstances. It is true power. If you'd like to get more in touch with your intuitive powers there's several ways that you can approach it.

A first step would be to hone your experiential intuition. Keep studying and learning all you can about the areas of your life's purpose and goals. Now there's a saying that says preparation plus opportunity equals luck, right? You know, some people call that an overnight success. I think it's because they fail to see that a person has studied long hours, labored, and sacrificed to achieve his or her goals. Doing this builds the hierarchy, the steps of the ladder that we talked about earlier. You never know when the new learning will come in handy.

Step 2, is to also work on trusting your more profound spiritual intuition. Open your heart and mind to its presence and learn to trust it completely. Recently in my mentorship program I was teaching a lesson on intuition and I said that most of us will reach out and ask God, call it the spiritual universe or infinite intelligence for help or guidance, and ask for a sign that we're on the right path. I think all of us have done that at some point in our life.

Then when we're driving down the road, we have one of those out of the blue experiences where bump, an idea pops into our mind. However, instead of embracing that thought and that idea, we question the source. We say, you know, are you sure? We kind of turn our heads to the heavens and say are you sure? We immediately start to doubt this guided or spiritual intuition. Then we begin to ask all the wrong questions. We ask is this a good idea or is this a bad idea? Should I do this or should I not do this? Is this right or is this wrong?

See the problem with those kinds of questions is that they are limiting by their very nature. The answer to all of those questions is it right or wrong, good or bad, should I or shouldn't I is yes. Right? If we look at it with just our reasoning mind it has to be just yes because that's the expression of the law of polarity. The law of polarity or the law of opposites tells us that, for instance every problem there's a solution. For up there's down. For left there's right. For good there's bad.

So, when we've asked God or this creative power to step into our lives and guide us and we are intuitively given the answer, remember what the late Wayne Dyer says. He says "if prayer is you talking to God, then your intuition is when God's answering you." So why are we questioning it? The law of opposites tells us that there are probably valid reasons why we should and why we shouldn't. Why we could and why we couldn't, right?

You know it was Socrates that said the quality of the questions we ask will ultimately determine the quality of the answers we get in our lives. So, here's my suggestion in Step 2 as we begin to develop trust in this profound spiritual intuition. When we open our hearts and minds to its presence and we learn to trust it completely. When we are gifted with an intuitive insight towards the next step in our life let's not ask the wrong or right or good or bad or should I or shouldn't I type questions. Instead let's ask this. If I act on this idea, will it move me closer to the dream that I claim I want in my life? Will this idea move me closer to co-creating the mental model of perfection that I claim I want in my life?

It's so simple yet our years of conditioning and formal education make it hard for people to accept. It's like Jim Carey's character in the movie Bruce Almighty where he's intensely praying to God for guidance and he speeds down the road in his car and there are explicit signs everywhere that he's going the wrong way, literally and figuratively. But he remains oblivious to the signs; he wrecks his car and ultimately his life.

At times we're often like that too. We ignore those signs around us. We ignore our own gut instincts and hunches. So, I urge you to open your mind and your heart and begin to trust your intuitive source and begin to ask more powerful questions when you're guided. Just as with intuition based on building real world knowledge, you build your spiritual trust day by day, month by month, with one application after the other. Now we should expect some fear and uncertainty at first, but have confidence and trust that God is in charge.

Once we are free from the uncertainty and self-doubt we begin to operate on a completely different level of awareness. What will happen is that over time you will begin to become free from your habitual conditioning and programmed thinking. Remember it's your willingness to shift your plane of awareness that is the precursor to every major change in your life. This is the very first decision you must make to unleash your spiritual intuitive factor.

You might first start by testing yourself in a very simple way. The next time you suddenly think of someone you haven't seen or heard from in a while, write down the day and time. Then call that person as soon as you can. Let them know that you were thinking of them at that particular time and place and see if that impression holds any significance or meaning. Likewise, the next time you get a hunch, follow it, and see what happens. I believe that by doing so as you begin to see results, outcomes and manifestations that are new, different and welcomed, you will begin to trust your intuitive power and will begin to become aware of your oneness with your infinite source.

As I said before this is not hocus-pocus and it might seem a little like magic to those who have not studied this concept before. If you will open your mind, if you will open your heart to this life power that you have been given, you will begin to see opportunities around you that you were never aware of before. Remember that even though it's essential to develop and access the power of your intuition, intuition is not a substitute for knowledge. If you have the wrong facts or are otherwise unprepared or unlearned then your intuition can be misinterpreted.

Ideally your intuition or subconscious mind should work in harmony with your analytical or conscious mind to provide a more holistic approach to decision making. This is one of the key reasons that I believe it's so important for a person to continue to study and to be committed to being a life-long learner.

The result of intuition is a shift in your awareness, your thoughts, and your actions. You will start to do things differently, you'll think differently, take different actions that are not necessarily in harmony at first with your habitual past and through this process you will begin to develop an inner level of comfort and security regardless of the challenges that confront you. Soon you'll be able to recognize moments and opportunities that will help you fulfill your life's purpose. Enjoy this power.

Intuition

NOTES

Leadership

Hello and welcome. I'm Michele Sfakianos and in this lesson, I'd like to examine Leadership as our eighth strategy – Leadership and its connection to living a successful and rewarding life.

I'm going to take a little bit of a non-traditional view because I don't believe leadership is just about the vision of where you see yourself or your organization. That's a mile-high view if you will. My mentor, John Maxwell said "all leaders cast vision. Good leaders put their team in the picture. Great leaders make them the center of the picture." To me this is really powerful.

Here is what I think he was getting at. Leadership comes from an internal process. A process of being willing to continually reinvent yourself and your organization to get that vision. Because in order to do something that you've never done you've got to become someone you've never been or at least something more than you've ever been. True leadership emerges from within. From our foundational values and not from apposition of power, wealth, association, or authority as it's often believed. It stems from holding strong convictions about one's inner truth and vision and beliefs and values.

It's important to realize that a leader isn't necessarily the smartest person, the most socially or professionally savvy, the tallest person or even the most well-liked person in the group. Those attributes are valuable but not necessary for leadership. Another common misconception is that to lead you must have followers. In truth the qualities of leadership are attributes of success and not those attributes of authority as I just described.

The late well-known professor of organizational behavior Dr. Bernard Bass said that people can become leaders through both circumstance and choice. Now this suggests that people can actually learn leadership. If you have the will and desire you can become an effective leader through a deliberate process of self-study, planning and hard work. You should know that your respect as a leader is not derived from your resume but rather from an observation of your actions, particularly those actions that define you as a person which are your passions, your motivations, your character, and your convictions. People want to know if you are honorable and trustworthy. Or if you're likely to be self-serving with their authority and trust.

Inevitably your leadership will be seen through their eyes as a reflection of what you know, what you do, and most importantly who you are. The type of leadership you practice should be based in honor of and with respect to your vision and life's purpose. As we've learned from the previous Strategies if you come from a place of authenticity the law of attraction ensures that you will attract the qualities that will build success and thereby further establish your ability to lead.

The late founder of Wal-Mart, Sam Walton provides an example of leadership on so many different levels. Most would agree that Walton was a leader who used his convictions, actions, and small-town sensibilities to achieve success beyond imagination. Under Sam Wal-Mart grew to be the largest employer in the United States and the world's largest revenue generating company. Sam Walton grew the company because he led with what he knew through his conviction and vision and he worked with dedicated commitment to propel his business forward.

His competitors have recalled how Sam used popcorn on the sidewalk in front of his store to lure people in with the smell. How he scoured their stores regularly and made sure he matched or beat their prices. How he mortgaged his family's home more than once and that was a great leap of faith, as he had a wife and four children to support. How he moved his stores away from the downtown and into suburban shopping mall locations that others paid so dearly for.

Sam Walton followed his own unique philosophy and vision. Rather than increase prices to increase profits, he cut costs and provided relief on bulk sales. Something his retail colleagues of the day thought was utterly ridiculous. Even in his late years as an elderly man with bone cancer ravaging through his body and causing him great physical pain, he continued to visit as many stores around the country to connect personally with and inspire his employees. He was asked about his success and he would reply, we're all working together, that's the secret. That's the "who" you are attributing great leadership. Leaders share the praise and recognize that no one does it alone. They believe in their vision, they act on it and they care for others, and in the process they ultimately inspire.

In fact, leadership can be defined as the capacity or ability to stimulate and induce action, guide, direct and inspire others to action. Do you know someone who possesses these leadership qualities? If you do, I suggest you take a moment now, just write down that person's name, and think about the ways in which he or she inspires you. Take a couple of minutes and maybe record or reflect upon your thoughts, and as you do think of how you can emulate those same leaders to inspire others in your life. List or think of at least two specific actions you can identify from the person you named.

Remember, leadership can be learned. You see, leaders inspire others through their invitation to a common cause or vision. A good leader can be a top-notch sales executive or it can be a small child leading others in a game. Those who have not studied or consciously thought about leadership may hold a distorted perception about it. Their concept most likely came from rock stars, athletes, entertainers, or those of means, and can't distinguish between a position of celebrity and one of leadership.

But as we mature most learn that leadership has little to do with fame, position, power, money, or intelligence. Instead it's an inner quality; almost a spiritual quality that does not change with circumstances. Leadership comes from a higher inner truth.

If you reflect on the leaders you've admired in your life, I believe you'll recognize other leadership characteristics as well. For instance, leaders don't need to tell people they're the leader. It's simply known. They lead by example through hard work and impeccable honesty and integrity. People know that they can trust them, so they come to believe in their vision also.

Remember what I said earlier, having followers is not required to lead? In fact, it might help us here to understand leadership by understanding followership. In the most familiar social context, the leader helps followers to find their voice. To be able to speak authentically and to be empowered to act upon what it is that they see and what needs to be done in the world. In effect, to be their own leader.

This type of followership or self-leadership is leadership nonetheless. And those qualities that we internalize and exemplify whether in full view of others or quietly on our own are the attributes necessary to achieve success. The practice of those attributes in your own life enables you to operate more effectively in the context of followership and empowers us to develop the leader within ourselves. It isn't the language of somebody should do something, as long as it's not going to be me, by contrast a leader is a problem-solver. Whether he or she caused the problem or not, he or she won't complain or whine to others. They won't pass the buck or point out reasons why things can't be done.

Leaders think about what needs to be done and what must be done and they take the responsibility for solving the problems. A leader steps forward and acts regardless of whether he or she is being followed. So how can you start to develop or hone these types of leadership skills? I've been taught and believe because I've seen it in action that there is a learning model upon which we can build these skills. But it doesn't stand alone. The learning that we acquire through this model needs to be plugged back in continuously. It is cyclical and begins with self-assessment.

First, as you've already started to do, observe and reflect on the attributes of the leaders in your life. Let them inspire you to be open to more opportunities, to new ideas and different ways of doing things. At the same time utilize the strategy lessons to help you identify your vision and life's purpose and allow your vision to define the point of view from where you will lead.

The second step in this cycle is self-approval. Give yourself permission to take on or embrace that challenge and go for it. Often what we do and what we achieve in our life is subconsciously what we believe we deserve or can do.

I spoke before about believing in the vision we have and that if we set a goal and we come from a place of honesty, others will be able to embrace it out of our trust a broader vision for themselves. They will not only see the possibility but the ability to achieve it.

Thirdly, acknowledge and commit to the next step, and the next and the next towards the goal. Einstein once said this "thinking has brought me this far and has created some problems that this thinking can't solve." With each new commitment it's about operating from a different place. About dying to who you've been and giving birth to who you must become. And ultimately, it's about doing the things that are required to operate at that new level of awareness. We often hear people say don't look back. It isn't that you shouldn't self-assess; we have a step for that. Rather commit as a leader about projecting the vision forward.

As commitment becomes achievement, we enter the fourth step of the cycle, self-fulfillment. Recognize the victories, both where we've been and where we've gotten to be and pat yourself and everybody on the team on their back. Then begin the process over again. Self-assessment, how did we get here? What is it that we need to discard? What do we need to keep? Self-approval, let's raise the bar and out of that comes commitment to another level of achievement and execution which comes with energy and focus. Then we realize self-fulfillment.

Finally, you go right back to self-assessment. How do we go higher and further? As you can see leadership, individually and collectively, evolves with time. With people involved and with yourself, it's a continuous process. And I think most important of all it's about an understanding that leadership is not about authority. It's about authenticity. Remember leaders are not only born, they can also be made. You can and must be your own life's leader.

NOTES

Faith

Hello and welcome. I'm Michele Sfakianos and in this lesson, I want to talk about strategy Number 9 Faith and the role of faith in living a successful and rewarding life.

You know 19th Century pastor, D.L. Moody worked with some in the nation's worst slums, and yet he observed that faith is the foundation of all society. We have only to look around us to see this. Now amidst the deplorable conditions and despairs that he encountered he saw people demonstrating kindness and exhibiting faith in their future. How could someone be experiencing despair exhibit faith in their future?

What is this kind of faith and where does it come from? In its simplest form, faith is complete trust or confidence in someone or something based on our strong belief rather than physical proof.

Faith is the means by which the unimaginable, untouchable and unknown becomes manifest in your life. It is the element of miracles. It is the most powerful unseen force in human nature and on a practical level it is the secret to success. Faith can never be touched or measured. Gravity does not affect it. And it works regardless of any other natural force, yet its impact on one's life can be so profound it is among the most crucial strategy you can employ.

Faith is subject to only one role that must be understood to harness its full power and that role is simply this. Whatever you repeat to yourself, no matter how unsubstantiated or untrue - it becomes your reality. Deliberate or habitual thoughts that you allow to stir in your mind forge

and create your life experience, and faith can be one of mind's most powerful and positive influences.

Faith is an inner knowing of what shall come, but also, it's a knowing
that grows and shows up in what you do. It's dynamic, not static. Most of
us have never cultivated our faith in ourselves, in our abilities or in the
application of our experiences. We have not cultivated our faith in the
things we believe and in the growing of that faith by experimenting with
risking, failing and succeeding again and again.

Think about it this way. Your awareness and belief system are what
got you to this point in your life. Unequivocally it is the basis of your
results. Now imagine what could happen once you understand the full
power of faith through your personal experience and how to direct and
harness it. Your results in life are what they are right now because of the
thoughts controlling your mind. It is well documented that people come
to believe whatever their reoccurring thoughts tell them and it makes no
difference whether these thoughts are true or false. You heard me right.
It makes no difference whether these thoughts are true or false.

If you've read this far, I know you want to be, do and have more and
fully develop your potential to build a successful rewarding life. The fact
that you are still here means that you can create a far greater and more
amazing life. What you may not realize is that the moment is now - and
recognizing the moment is key. It's the difference between mediocrity and
greatness.

When Dr. Martin Luther King said I have a dream that was different
than the average Joe saying I have a dream. Because of his experiences,
his vision and the things he had done, there were things people felt from
his mountaintop speech which came from his faith. It came from that

place of faith from which he spoke. From which he allowed us to see the future through his eyes. His was a dimension of faith that most people do not experience because they have never allowed their faith to flow from a belief in themselves and their work, their skills and the rightness of the direction of their vision - A direction that will allow them to have break-throughs.

I'm now speaking to that more infinite you that can be awakened through the power of faith, one of the most powerful forces in the universe. True faith in yourself, in your creator and higher power can harness and bring forth greater achievement than whatever you might imagine on your own. I'd like to make a distinction here. Have you ever watched the movie or read the book "The Secret?" I differ from my colleagues in the movie "The Secret" on one point. I don't think that we should limit ourselves and our practice of faith to just the material world, thinking about the house that we want to live in or the sunny beach vacation that lasts forever or the Ferrari or whatever toys we may want.

I believe we can and should have our faith practice with a much grander vision, like Martin Luther King did. What we can give; what we can create; how we can contribute and then have faith that we can bring these things into reality. The cars and toys and vacations will ultimately follow, but let's not limit our faith practice to just the material goods. You know some people would define the word ethics as values in action. I believe accomplishments are faith in action. They are measured in terms of how much good, how much service, and how well you solve difficulties. You know, I have the faith that you are fully equipped to bring forth these life contributions in whatever areas that speaks to you.

Of course, you'll need to use your skills, your creativity, your passion, and your love to do it, but the moment you understand the concept and power of faith I have no doubt that you will be guided in their use and life will compensate you for it. You've probably heard the story of the woman who prayed each night to win the lottery so that she could help her family and her community. She'd pray, you know it's not for me Lord, I want to use the money for others. And night after night she prayed her faith strong that one day her prayers would be answered, but they weren't.

Finally, one night after she said her prayer with its usual sincerity and faith, she was startled to hear the voice of God. "Night after night you have prayed, but to fulfill your prayer you must meet me halfway. Go and buy the ticket!" I think we've all heard similar stories. That really is the way of faith. You cannot expect riches and fulfillment to suddenly drop in on you from the sky. You must act in ways to make them happen. And if you protest that you can't do it alone have faith that assistance will come to help you so that you can manifest it. Once you begin to move forward on faith, you will find that there are a number of people who are more than qualified to assist you in your work. It is your faith in what you can be and what you can contribute that must be your driving force.

As with any of the strategy faith is a skill that can be cultivated and perfected. We can push aside our justifications and rationalizations and skepticisms regarding the things unknown and unseen, if we believe, if we have faith in our vision and purpose that becomes our reality. Such deep faith is a state of mind that can be cultivated, and to begin to cultivate the power of faith in your life I suggest you start by paying attention to the negative thoughts that creep in and occupy your waking hours.

Notice the times you are internally complaining, judging, feeling inadequate or down. Notice the time you spend criticizing yourself. You know the first step can be very uncomfortable, but it's vitally important for you to be aware of the amount of thought, power and energy you waste on a daily basis with this kind of thinking. Consciously or subconsciously this thought stream is generating sensations and emotions in your body and these naturally attract more of the same.

I cannot stress enough how important it is to be vigilant of your state of being. Your thoughts, your feelings, emotions, because regardless of whether they're good or bad, desirable or undesirable, healthy or unhealthy, they are like a magnet that attract other energies of the same kind. Once you've disciplined your mind to extend positive energy and vibrations you can begin the three-step process to manifest your vision through faith.

First, establish a crystal clear image or statement of your desired outcome. Visualize it completely. Write your outcome out using action verbs like I am, I can, or I will.

Second, allow yourself to be filled with an intense almost overwhelming stream of sincere emotion about the desired outcome. In other words, feel the joy and satisfaction that will come as you move toward and achieve your vision one step at a time. Think of how rewarding and how satisfying it will be for you and others.

Third, take deliberate physical action steps toward your desired outcome. This is so critical. Just as you did with your vision you must write down specific actions you can take to realize and manifest your faith. Know that the ideas that happen to spring in your mind are not there by accident. They are faith beginning to be realized. These three steps empower us to create the reality that may have previously seemed impossible. It works because the desired outcome is understood with a new clarity and then our emotion touches us at an inner level and helps us feel our intense desire and result in joy.

And our actions, like buying a lottery ticket move us toward the actual realization. You know I have found that this simple process is the recipe for manifesting anything we really want in our lives. Of course, this is not a process that I came up with. More than a century ago Wallace D. Wattles wrote a book, The Science of Getting Rich. In there he says something really profound. He said "Faith is the crucial juncture where thought and personal action must be combined." You cannot simply give your creative impulse to original substance and then sit down and wait for results. He said "If you do, you will never get them. You must act. There is never a time but now and there never will be any time but now. If you are ever to make ready for the reception of what it is that you want", he said "You must begin now."

You know, that is beautiful. This is something you should write down and post everywhere you can see it. Again, he said: "If you do, you will never get them. You must act. There is never a time but now and there never will be any time but now. If you are ever to make ready for the reception of what it is that you want", he said "You must begin now." See, this is the faith that I'm talking about. It's not simply wishing up a star, but wishing upon a star with such intense passion that you have an unstoppable conviction to take action. Each of the components of faith's triad, image, emotion, and action naturally feeds the other until the force becomes so overwhelming that you can't help but manifest the object of your desired outcome.

Remember that our human heritage is a living testament to faith's power. Just look at the great spiritual leader Gandhi who with no clothing, money, army took on the British empire and won impressing upon countless others the power of a non-violence. Think about the two Ohio brothers of modest means named Wilbur and Orville Wright who decided they wanted to fly and did it making the world forever smaller. Consider the relative handful of humans who were determined to go to the moon and in doing so, Neil Armstrong and Buzz Aldrin forever changed the way we see our blue planet.

History has shown us time and time again that what seems to be impossible can be achieved through faith. Faith is the willingness to know that even when you have given everything you have and things still don't work out you don't bow. You don't beat yourself up. You understand at a very deep level that it's not over yet. Your faith is continuously being developed through its application. It's the patience, the willingness to do what is required, even when you have no evidence to support it. You're hanging in there when you can't see the light at the end of the tunnel when all the odds say there's no possibility you can make this happen. There's a sense within yourself that says I must stand. This is what I must do and this is what I believe.

Like Dr. Martin Luther King, while the results might not manifest until you've left the planet, you'll know that you stood for something. That you believed it. You operated with the spirit of integrity and you can leave here taking your last breath content in the victory of achieving your life's purpose.

When I first started to become a speaker and enter into this field of personal development, faith helped me attract the right people. The right situations put me in the right environment for my dream to motivate others so that they can live their best life. You know, I worked hard. I took deliberate actions to create the right conditions on the physical play, but I didn't have a guarantee of a fulfilled promise. But my faith kept me working, even when the external result seemed few. Miracles or grace, call it what you will, these are the results of faith.

Today, not a moment goes by without my being grateful, truly grateful for the blessings that have been manifested in my life. Once I was able to pierce and see past the barriers, once I was able to lift confusions veil and express my vision clearly and with emotional sincerity, I could take action steps with passion and faith and proceed with greater and greater ease.

You can do this! You can achieve far greater results if you choose. Remember clear your mind of negativity and become absolutely clear on what it is that you want.

Focus on what you want to do and how you're going to contribute to others. Once you've developed the picture, run the image in your mind like a movie and become emotionally involved in it. Allow yourself to bathe in the sensations of accomplishment, success, happiness, gratitude, and love. Let the images and the emotions overwhelm you. Put on some music or videos or anything else that can deepen the emotion and bring your images into focus. From that state get up and take your first step through faith toward making your vision come true.

No matter how small or large the first step is, do it. You might want to also involve others in the form of a support system. Have faith in yourself and recruit others to have faith in you. Let others know what your goals and dreams are. Let them see your passion for success. Also let them see your preparation and effort.

One of the things I do is I share my dreams with my family and friends and their faith creates both accountability and a vibration that goes to work on my behalf. I continue to develop and elevate my level of awareness through engaging in seminars and life coaching. The love, support and inspiration are a key source of personal and intellectual growth for me. It strengthens my faith in the rightness of the work and gives me an opportunity to share my faith with others to help them achieve their dreams as well.

I've found that being supportive in this way is especially helpful if our positive state begins to shift. When your sincere belief is blended with the positive emotion and support of others the universe conspires in your favor. It's the law, and this is true faith. It has been said that faith is not believing that God can, but believing that God will. Have faith in your vision, your higher power, and yourself. Don't allow your fears to derail you. Have faith, courage and persistence and when the time is right your faith will be rewarded in more ways than you can possibly imagine.

Faith

NOTES

Hello and welcome. This is Michele Sfakianos and I'd like to focus this last lesson in this strategy book on giving.

Before I go into this last strategy, I would like to take a moment to review the last nine strategies.

1. Understanding - When we expand our awareness of our infinite true potential; when we challenge the convictions of our old limiting beliefs and replace them with new empowering beliefs; when we gain a true understanding of who we are and, more importantly, whose we are and apply the Strategies in our lives, we will never again be held in the field of limitation of what we currently have and see for our lives.

2. Honesty - As a daily practice, gauge your levels of openness with yourself, with others, and with your hopes, your dreams, your intentions, and your actions throughout the day and see how your practice of honesty can be deepened.

3. Vision - The vision that you create for yourself, and over the years you'll have many, must be clear that you bring it into your consciousness easily, like Kennedy's vision of reaching the moon. Vision serves as the connector between your life's purpose and the goals you will set to realize it. As you continue, you will see how all the Strategies will provide an awareness of all of your resources, strategies, and tactics to further strengthen your own vision, life's purpose, and resolve.

4.   Persistence - I shared with you this: your habits are what define your hours, your days, and your life. Your habits will define how you persist towards your final goals and your achievements. Remember that persistence is not a burden - but a blessing. Hold on and keep going. Stick to your vision and soon it will be realized.

5.   Focus - Focus will allow you to conserve energy, time, and resources by harnessing your power to follow the critical path to success. Emerson said this, "Where your focus goes, your energy flows." If your focus is in a thousand different directions, then your energy is scattered, weakened, and disorganized. Your focus on these Strategies is a positive step toward directing your energy and concentrating its power on what really matters to you: which should be living your life's purpose.

6.   Courage – We talked about a well-known author, photographer, and Buddhist monk, Matthieu Ricard, who said: "It's not the magnitude of the task that matters; it's the magnitude of our courage." So, be courageous as you go and grow forward. It will make all the difference in achieving success.

7.   Intuition - The result of intuition is a shift in your awareness, your thoughts, and your actions. You will start to do things differently, you'll think differently, take different actions that are not necessarily in harmony at first with your habitual past and through this process you will begin to develop an inner level of comfort and security regardless of the challenges that confront you. Soon you'll be able to recognize moments and opportunities that will help you fulfill your life's purpose.

8.   Leadership - Leadership, individually and collectively, evolves with time. With the involvement of other people and yourself, it's a continuous process. And I think most important of all it's about an

understanding that leadership is not about authority. It's about authenticity. Remember leaders are not only born, they can also be made. You can and must be your own life's leader.

9. Faith - When your sincere belief is blended with the positive emotion and support of others the universe conspires in your favor. It's the law, and this is true faith. It has been said that faith is not believing that God can, but believing that God will. Have faith in your vision, your higher power, and yourself. Don't allow your fears to derail you. Have faith, courage and persistence and when the time is right your faith will be rewarded in more ways than you can possibly imagine.

Now let's move onto strategy #10 - Giving. We are familiar with the saying such as give to get or give and you shall receive. Many people make their giving decisions with the thought that I'll give to be in good standing or I'll give because what I put out comes back to me. This all sounds a lot like bargaining to me rather than real giving.

See, giving is not something like the telethon where you get a tote bag in return for your pledge. Nor, is it like buying a raffle ticket from the local Boy Scout chapter for the possibility of winning a car. The giving I'll be talking about in this lesson is an act of the heart, demonstrating all the virtues of the heart, generosity, love, faith, & gratitude. The act of giving from the heart cannot be separated from its intentions or motivations.

To start, this means that you don't give with the purpose of getting something in return. One motivation of giving from the heart is the full recognition and thankfulness for all that we have. In this way giving is the result of focusing on our true wealth, in every area of our lives from which we can give. With this type of giving you will not only be nurturing gratitude; you'll be nurturing trust. Trust that you will always have more than what it is that you want so you can always afford to give more to others.

Give and you shall receive not because God or some universal power will someday reward you for the goodness and kindness you've extended. Give because in the very moment that you offer kindness and goodness you become transformed instantaneously. Your entire being begins to move to the vibration of gratitude. It has been said that giving is like a perfume. You can't sprinkle it on others without getting a few drops on yourself.

The moment you give truly from your heart there is an immediate and profound sense of wellness and goodness. This is such a satisfying and harmonious state to be in. Yet few people allow themselves the time to really live and come from this place. Instead they forego the true rewards of giving because they are expecting something in return.

Bob Berg wrote a wonderful book called the Go Giver that speaks on this idea as a foundational law in business and as a way of life in every area of our lives. The premise of Bob's book is that we need to be relentless go givers. See when you give you enter into the vibration of something greater than yourself and you become aligned with the replenishing laws of the universe, and the universe responds in overwhelming fashion, as though a million invisible hands are at work on your behalf.

Circumstances change; the attitude of those around you change; and your outlook changes. In short through giving from your heart you are in line with the working forces of nature and will operate in its most func-tional productive and rewarding state. After all giving is a part of human nature. It's necessary for our very survival. When I look back at my own life now, I realize that every opportunity that I've been given was a result of someone giving in some form or fashion to me.

When we witness an act of true giving whether we are the giver, the receiver or the observer of the act, we are filled with warmth, smiles and at times we're even moved to tears. An excellent illustration is the HGTV show Extreme Home Makeovers. We can see giving in a way that changes someone's life forever it energizes the entire community and infuses the television audience with those same emotions.

Few know how to give and fewer know how to light themselves up through giving. Most everyone else seems to just bargain. In our hearts we know when we've given, and when we've been bargained to give. As Maya Angelo pointed out the sensation of true giving is profound. The only reason many people won't allow themselves to give in this way is fear. This may be the reason some don't experience the liberating joy that arises from true giving.

So, what are some of the obstacles placed in our path that feed our fear and hinder our giving? The first is self-concern. We tend to be over-whelmed with our own wants and needs demands that are placed upon our time and finances and by our own obligations. Now many of us may want to dismiss this point. But to clearly to focus on these immediate needs is not selfish, however that doesn't mean that giving should stop.

We waste so much of our energy, so much of our creative resources with worrying about where our good is coming from. You know - how are we going to have enough? How can we get more? That we literally rob ourselves of the abundant unrestricted life that is seeking to be expressed if we would just live in harmony and an awareness of the law that governs its flow.

I would argue that for this reason it is in times of our greatest crisis that giving may be all the more essential. I know not all of us are in a position to give materially, but we can give of our time and talents. If truth be told we could even give some financial support. Either way, sacrificial giving sends the signal to the universe that we recognize the gifts we have. That we're grateful for what we have and that we have faith that there is more in store for us.

It demonstrates our intention to play a role in the productive force of mankind. More importantly we send the signal that we believe in ourselves and in God to the extent that our wants and needs will be met. See, I believe that giving is a covenant between us and God. That we give what we have and what is of value to us and that we are promised that it will come back 100-fold.

Now, we don't get to dictate the terms of the return. That again is just bargaining. But we can have faith that we will receive whatever it is that we need in ways that we can't even anticipate. This brings me to the second obstacle of giving - A lack of faith. In our previous lesson on faith I go into this topic in more detail. But I want to discuss it briefly here in the context of giving.

Your source of blessings is not from yourself, but from God, and the literal give and take of his work in others. In the Bible in Luke 6:38 the Sermon on the Mount lays the foundation for this concept. In one of its most quoted verses mankind is told "Give and it shall be given unto you. Good measure pressed down and shaken together and running over. For with this same measure that you give, it shall be measured to you again."

You see, to refrain from giving is to overlook this truth and trust only in ourselves and not in the promise that has been made to us. If we cannot trust in anything bigger than ourselves then we will be less likely to give, and we should not then expect to receive anything bigger than ourselves. Everything we experience and create in our life is an expression of our awareness. From our current awareness we form a habit of thinking. That forms a habit of doing and that ultimately creates the habit of our being.

If your being is in any way feeling limited at any level, not just financially and that's important to understand, limited in any way what giving does is it shifts your awareness. It will alter it in ways that nothing else will. It will alter your entire being's vibration and this new vibration will, over time, move in harmony with the vibration of abundance. The vibration and expectation of abundance is also a mindset and is directly opposite of scarcity from which we tend to look at the world. It too requires a shift of our awareness, a recognition that you come from an infinite source instead of limiting conditions and circumstances.

When you step into your infinite potentiated self you begin to come from, live from, think from, and give from this infinite source. This shift in awareness and vibration will alter your self-belief in ways that produce results you cannot even begin to predict and your cup will truly run over. So, give right now. Pick up the phone and call someone. Offer a kind and sincere phrase to someone you love. Make a difference to a stranger. Give of your true talents. Give and you give yourself the greatest gift of all.

The world will respond in kind, not because of some magical and unseen force but because you have become transformed and therefore you begin to attract the qualities that you seek and the ripple effect is created. Your circumstances will never again dictate that you can't have a life beyond what you currently have.

So, stop looking in conditions and circumstances for your how. Your how is not there. Your how is in you and the way you choose to live your life. Changing our focus from what we are getting to how we are giving will cause us to live our lives in a completely different way; in harmony with the needs and wants of others and in balance with your own needs and desires.

In some way our need for love, friendship, or satisfaction in the workplace dictates what we should give. Don't let your need define your solution. Apply reverse logic so you can set your goals based solely upon what it is that you want to give. Doing this allows us to become the vibrational match for the outcome that we want to create.

You will find that you are more creative in business and more alert to financial and personal opportunities. Because you've heightened your awareness of the world around you and you are now in harmony with it. The result is that you will literally have a new depth to your productivity and creativeness because your outcome is now unlimited.

No matter what your circumstances are if you practice abundant giving you become fully equipped to enjoy the liberty provided by your infinite source, and you can just watch the ripples grow.

You know, without a doubt the understanding I received from these strategies and then applying them into my life has been critical to my highest achievement. I really hope that these strategies will help you live your dream and achieve your life's purpose, whatever that may be.

NOTES

Index

About the Author

MICHELE SFAKIANOS (Sfa-can-iss) is a Registered Nurse, Leading Authority on Parenting and Life Skills, Speaker, Certified Personal Coach and an Award-winning Author. Her books and programs provide the answers you've always wanted to many of life's difficult "who/what/why/where/when and how-to" questions. Her experience as a Registered Nurse, mother and grandmother, along with her extensive training qualifies her as an expert in her field. Michele has two college degrees (Nursing and Computer Programming) and several certifications (Personal Coaching, Legal Nursing, Copywriting and Real Estate).

She has won many awards for her books including: 2012 Indie Excellence Winner; 2012 Gold Medal Living Now Book Awards; 2013 Bronze Medal Readers' Favorite Book Award; 2013 Gold Medal Wise Bear Digital Book Awards; and multiple Honorable Mentions. Michele has the desire to help others reach their full potential by providing information in a concise, direct-to-the-point, manner. She knows your time is valuable and strives to provide you the information you need, quickly and accurately, to unlock your potential. Let Michele help you to be the success you were meant to be!

Open Pages Publishing is a self-publishing company offering books to inspire, teach, and inform readers. We specialize in a variety of subjects including: life skills, self-help, reference, parenting, leadership and teens.

Ordering Information:

Open Pages Publishing books are available at major online bookstores. They may also be purchased for educational, business, or promotional use.

For bulk orders: special discounts are available on bulk orders. For details contact our sales staff at info@openpagespublishing.com.

Visit openpagespublishing.com for a list of books by
Michele Sfakianos

www.ingramcontent.com/pod-product-compliance
Lightning Source LLC
LaVergne TN
LVHW051422080426
835508LV00022B/3206